The River Thames shaped and sired London. But for centuries the life- giving water posed a deadly threat through flooding. Now, the Thames Barrier at Woolwich Reach guards the vulnerable heart of London from abnormally high tides.

The Barrier consists of 10 separate pivoting steel gates strung out in a 520 metre line across the river. In normal conditions, ships pass between the gates but when warnings are given, the protective barrier can swing into place within 30 minutes to block the threatening water from surging up the Thames.

Die Themse zeugte und formte London. Das lebensspendende Wasser bedrohte die Stadt jedoch jahrhundertelang mit gefährlichen Überschwemmungen. Heute schützt die Hochwassersperre (Thames Barrier) bei Woolwich Reach den verletzlichen Kern der Stadt vor abnormal hohen Gezeiten.

Die Sperre besteht aus 10 Stahltoren, die getrennt geschwenkt werden und in einer 520 m langen Linie über den Fluß verteilt sind. Bei normalem Wasserstand fahren Schiffe zwischen den Toren hindurch, die dann aber innerhalb von 30 Minuten in Schutzstellung gedreht werden können und dem gefährlichen Flutwasser den Weg versperren, sobald eine Hochwasserwarnung gegeben wird.

La Tamise tisse ses méandres à travers Londres. Et pourtant, pendant des siècles, le fleuve qui donna la vie à Londres sema aussi la mort à cause des inondations. Désormais, la barrière de la Tamise à Woolwich Reach protège le coeur vulnérable de Londres contre les marées hautes anormales.

Elle consiste en 10 barrières d'acier pivotantes alignées à intervalles sur 520 mètres en travers du fleuve. Dans des conditions normales, les navires peuvent passer entre les barrières, mais dès que les avertissements sont affichés, la barrière de protection peut pivoter en place.

D0572421

The River Thames has been used continuously as a highway since prehistoric times. Along its banks, vast areas of London docks were built in the 19th century to berth ships bringing cargoes from around the world. The warehouses fell derelict in the latter half of the 20th century. Now **Docklands** has been regenerated into an extensive waterscape setting for new offices, businesses, shopping and watersport facilities, homes, heritage trails, a light railway and airport.

Canary Wharf is a vast commercial city, dubbed "Wall Street on the Water" which features a central tower taller than any other building in Britain.

Die Themse dient schon seit prähistorischer Zeit ununterbrochen als ein wichtiger Verkehrsweg. An ihrem Ufer wurden im 19. Jahrhundert riesige Flächen als Docks zum Anlegen von Schiffen, die Güter aus aller Welt brachten, ausgebaut. Die Lager standen in der zweiten Hälfte des 20. Jahrhunderts meist leer und verfielen. In jüngster Zeit wurden die **Docklands** jedoch zu einem großflächigen Gebiet mit neuen Büros, Geschäften und Läden.

Depuis les temps préhistoriques, la Tamise est utilisée comme voie de communication. Le long de ses rives, les vastes quartiers des docks londoniens furent construits au 19e siècle pour le mouillage des navires apportant leurs cargos de tous les coins du monde. Les entrepôts sont tombés en ruines dans la deuxième moitié du 20e siècle. On voit maintenant une nouvelle vie s'insuffler dans *les docks* dont la mise en valeur les a transformés en plans d'eau où se regroupent nouveaux bureaux, magasins, et centres commerciaux.

Canary Wharf est un vaste complexe financier, désigné comme le "Wall Street des eaux".

Greenwich is a memorial to the maritime might of Britain. The National Maritime Museum, containing records and relics of 500 years of naval history, is based in the elegant Queen's House, designed by Inigo Jones in 1616. Four square on the river's edge is the Royal Naval College designed by Sir Christopher Wren and built three hundred years ago.

The Cutty Sark, a Victorian sailing clipper, is in dry dock on the river bank.

Greenwich ist ein Denkmal an die Seemacht Großbritanniens. Das National Maritime Museum (Marinemuseum) im eleganten Queen's House enthält Aufzeichnungen und Relikte aus 500 Jahren Marine. Das Queen's House wurde 1616 von Inigo Jones entworfen. Direkt am Flußufer ist das Royal Naval College, Flußufer ist das Royal Naval College, das von Sir Christopher Wren entworfen und vor dreihundert Jahren gebaut wurde.

Greenwich est un monument commémorant la puissance maritime de la Grande-Bretagne. Le National Maritime Museum (Musée de la marine) qui contient les archives et les reliques de 500 années d'histoire navale, est logé dans l'élégante Queen's House, palais dessiné en 1616 par Inigo Jones. Tout au bord du fleuve se dresse le Royal Naval College, dessiné par Sir Christopher Wren et construit il y a trois cents ans.

Tower Bridge, the most famous and distinctive bridge in London, stands sentinel over the Thames. Between its twin gothic-style towers are the drawbridges which are raised in a minute and a half to allow ships to pass up river.

Between Tower Bridge and London Bridge - the city's oldest - is moored HMS Belfast which saw active service in World War II and is now a floating museum.

Tower Bridge, die berühmteste und bekannteste Brücke Londons, hält Wacht über die Themse. Zwischen ihren beiden Türmen im gothischen Stil befinden sich die Zugbrücken, die zum Freigeben der Durchfahrt von Schiffen innerhalb von eineinhalb Minuten geöffnet werden können.

Tower Bridge, le pont le plus célèbre et le plus remarquable de Londres, monte la garde au-dessus du fleuve. Entre ses deux tours gothiques, les ponts basculants se lèvent en une minute et demie pour laisser les navires remonter le fleuve.

The City is London's financial and commercial heartland. It has been bustling with businessmen since Roman times and occupies a site, "the Square Mile", virtually regarded as the entire area of early London. The City embraces the Bank of England in Threadneedle Street, the vaults of which house the nation's gold reserves; the Stock Exchange and the insurance institution, Lloyds of London.

The Mansion House is the official residence of the Lord Mayor of London, who provides pomp and pageantry each year when he rides in a State coach to the Law Courts - a ceremony which dates back to the 14th century.

Die City ist Londons Finanz- und Wirtschaftszentrum. Schon in römischen Zeiten wimmelte es hier von Geschäftsleuten. Die City befindet sich an einem Punkt, der praktisch als die gesamte Fläche des alten Londons betrachtet wird, der "Square Mile". Sie umfaßt die Bank of England in Threadneedle Street, deren Tresore die Goldreserven des Landes enthalten, die Börse (Stock Exchange) und das Versicherungsunternehmen Lloyds of London.

La City est le moteur financier et commercial de Londres. Depuis l'époque romaine, elle est fréquentée par les hommes d'affaires,et occupe un site, le "Square Mile", qui est considéré comme représentant la superficie toute entière de l'ancienne Londres. La City englobe la Banque d'Angleterre sise dans Threadneedle Street, dont les coffres contiennent les réserves d'or de la nation; le Stock Exchange et l'établissement d'assurances, Lloyds of London.

This massive walled fortress on the banks of the Thames was built more than 900 years ago to dominate and defend London.

The Tower of London is not a single building, rather a collection of fortresses, clustered round the great square White Tower.

Nearly a thousand years of history can be traced in these buildings which have served as home to kings, prison and grisly place of execution where queens and politicians, bishops and traitors, spies and statesmen have met their end.

Visitors can see the priceless collection of Crown Jewels, historic arms, armour and weapons, fearsome instruments of torture and the Yeoman warders in their colourful uniform.

Diese massive, von Mauern umschlossene Festung am Themseufer wurde vor mehr als 900 Jahren zur Beherrschung und zum Schutz von London erbaut.

Der Tower von London ist kein einzelnes Gebäude, sondern eher eine Ansammlung von Festungen, die sich um den großen, quadratischen White Tower drängen.

In diesen Bauwerken lassen sich nahezu tausend Jahre Geschichte zurückverfolgen: sie dienten als Königsburg, als Gefängnis und als gräulicher Hinrichtungsort, an dem Königinnen und Politiker, Bischöfe und Verräter, Spione und Staatsmänner den Tod fanden.

Besucher können hier die unschätzbar wertvolle Sammlung von Kronjuwelen, sowie historische Wappen, Rüstungen und Waffen, furchterregende Folterinstrumente und die Wärter in ihren farbenfrohen Uniformen betrachten.

Cette forteresse massive entourée de remparts, sise sur la rive de la Tamise, fut construite il y a plus de neuf cents ans pour dominer et défendre Londres.

La Tour de Londres n'est pas constituée d'un seul bâtiment, mais de plusieurs forteresses, agglutinées autour de la grande tour carrée: la Tour blanche.

On peut retrouver les traces de près de mille ans d'histoire dans ces bâtiments, qui ont servi de résidence aux rois, de prison et de sinistre lieu d'exécution où périrent reines, hommes politiques, évêques, traîtres, espions et hommes d'état.

Les visiteurs peuvent y voir la collection inestimable des joyaux de la Couronne, d'armes historiques, d'armures et d'instruments de torture redoutables, ainsi que les hallebardiers de la garde, dans leur uniforme coloré.

The Elizabethan **Globe Theatre**, opened in 1599, was burnt down in 1613 and rebuilt, only to be closed by the Puritans in 1642. Now a faithful reproduction of the first Globe Theatre stands just 200 yards from its original site on Bankside.

The reconstructed circular theatre has 20 wooden bays, each three storeys high. These, like the stage, are thatched.

During the summer, plays by Shakespeare and other contemporary dramatists such as Christopher Marlowe are performed at The Globe, where a permanent exhibition gives insight into life and work in Elizabethan England.

Das 1599 eröffnete elisabethanische **Globe Theatre** fiel 1613 einem Brand zum Opfer und wurde neu aufgebaut, jedoch 1642 von den Puritanern wieder geschlossen. Eine detailgetreie Reproduktion des ersten Globe Theatre steht jetzt nur 180m neben seiner ehemaligen Stätte an der Bankside.

Dieses rekonstruierte, kreisförmige Theater besitzt 20 hölzerne Nischen, und jede von ihnen ist dreistöckig. Wie die Bühne tragen auch sie ein Strohdach.

Während der Sommermonate werden Stücke von Shakespeare und anderen Dramatikern seines Zeitalters im Globe aufgeführt. Eine permanente Ausstellung vermittelt Einblick in das Leben und die Arbeit im elisabethanischen England.

Le théâtre élisabéthain du **Globe**, ouvert en 1599, fut détruit par un incendie en 1613, puis reconstruit, avant d'être fermé par les puritains en 1642. Aujourd'hui, une reproduction fidèle du premier théâtre du Globe se dresse à seulement 200 mètres de son site d'origine, sur la rive.

Le théâtre circulaire reconstruit contient vingt travées en bois, chacune de trois étages. Comme la scène, elles sont recouvertes d'un toit de chaume.

En été, les pièces de Shakespeare et de ses contemporains dramaturges sont jouées au Globe, où une exposition permanente donne un aperçu de la vie et des métiers dans l'Angleterre élisabéthaine.

St Paul's has an indomitable dignity and grandeur which inspires the nation at moments of great solemnity. There has been a Cathedral here since 604 AD.

When the previous building on the site was damaged in the Great Fire of London in 1666, Sir Christopher Wren designed the present Baroque-style replacement.

Seat of the Bishop of London and 'parish church' of the Commonwealth, the Cathedral is crowned by a central dome which rises some 120 metres.

St Paul's hat eine unbezwingbare Würde und Erhabenheit, die das britische Volk in Augenblicken großer Feierlichkeit inspirieren. An dieser Stelle steht schon seit 604 AD eine Kathedrale.

Als das vorherige Gebäude im Großen Feuer von London im Jahr 1666 beschädigt wurde, entwarf Sir Christopher Wren die heutige Kathedrale im barocken Stil.

St. Paul possède une dignité et une grandeur indomptable qui inspire la nation dans ses moments de grande solennité. Une cathédrale est érigée à cet endroit depuis l'an 604.

Quand le bâtiment érigé précédemment en ce lieu fut dévasté par le Grand Incendie de 1666, Sir Christopher Wren dessina le remplacement de style baroque actuel.

The Houses of Parliament, built in 1840 on the site of a former royal palace, are steeped in pomp and tradition, ceremony and splendour. The Clock Tower is popularly known as Big Ben, which is actually the name of the bell which strikes. A light in the tower shows when the House of Commons is in session.

The House of Lords is a lavishly decorated chamber containing the throne of the sovereign and the Woolsack, seat of the Lord Chancellor. The House of Commons' chamber for elected Members of Parliament was rebuilt in 1950 following war damage.

Die Houses of Parliament (dt. Parlamentsgebäude) wurden 1840 an dieser Stätte erbaut, auf der sich früher ein königlicher Palast befand. Sie sind reich an Gepränge und Tradition. Der Uhrenturm ist allgemein als "Big Ben" bekannt, obwohl Big Ben eigentlich der Name der Glocke ist, die die Stunden schlägt.

Das House of Lords (Oberhaus) ist ein reichverzierter Saal mit dem Thron des Monarchen und dem "Wollsack", dem Sitz des Lordkanzlers. Das Unterhaus für die gewählten Abgeordneten wurde 1950 neu erbaut, da es durch Luftangriffe beschädigt worden war.

Le Parlement, construit en 1840 sur le site d'un ancien palais royal, est imprégné de pompe et de tradition, de cérémonie et de splendeur. La tour de l'horloge est connue populairement sous le nom de "Big Ben", mais c'est en fait le nom de la cloche qui sonne les heures.

La Chambre des lords est une salle richement sculptée contenant le trône du souverain. La Chambre des communes pour les membres élus du Parlement a été reconstruite en 1950 à la suite des dégâts subis pendant la guerre.

The largest observation wheel in the world overhangs the River Thames near the southern end of Westminster Bridge. **London Eye**, built to celebrate the Millennium, stands stark against the skyline with its 32 observation pods ready to take passengers on a 30-minute trip high above the city. As the 135-metre- (450-ft) high wheel slowly rotates, a breathtaking all-round view, extending 25 miles across the city and beyond, is revealed.

Das größte Aussichtsrad der Welt hängt am Südende der Westminster Bridge über der Themse. Das zur Feier der Jahrtausendwende gebaute **London Eye** mit seinen 32 Aussichtskabinen, die bereitstehen, Fahrgäste zu einer 30-minütigen Rundfahrt hoch über der Stadt aufzunehmen, hebt sich krass von der Skyline ab. Die Fahrt im 135 Meter hohen Riesenrad enthüllt einen atemberaubenden Panoramablick, der sich 40 Kilometer über die Stadt und weiter erstreckt.

La tour d'observation la plus grande du monde domine la Tamise, près du côté sud du pont de Westminster. L'*Œil de Londres*, construit pour célébrer le millénaire, se dresse contre l'horizon, avec ses 32 nacelles d'observation, prêt à emporter ses passagers pour un voyage de 30 minutes au-dessus de la ville. Lorsque la roue de 135 mètres de haut commence à tourner lentement, un panorama époustouflant apparaît, sur plus de 40 kilomètres.

No church in Britain has been so closely connected with the nation's history as **Westminster Abbey**. Coronations of sovereigns spanning 900 years have been held here and most of them are buried within its walls. The Abbey Chapter House was the meeting place of early parliaments.

Small portions of the building date back to the 11th century; the choir and sanctuary are 13th century; the nave 15th century and the chapel early 16th century.

Keine Kirche in Großbritannien ist so eng mit der Geschichte der Nation verbunden wie **Westminster Abbey**. Monarchen aus neun Jahrhunderten wurden hier gekrönt, und die meisten von ihnen sind hier auch begraben. Das Abbey Chapter House war Sitzungsort der ersten Parlamente.

Kleine Teile des Gebäudes stammen aus dem 11. Jahrhundert.

Aucune église de Grande-Bretagne n'a été aussi étroitement liée à l'histoire de la nation que **l'abbaye de Westminster**. Depuis 900 ans, c'est là qu'ont lieu les couronnements des souverains dont la plupart sont enterrés dans ses murs. La salle du chapitre abrita les réunions des premiers parlements.

Des petites parties de l'édifice remontent au 11e siècle.

Westminster Cathedral for Roman Catholic worshippers was started in 1895 and designed by John Francis Bentley in the Byzantine style. Its striking red brick exterior is striped with white stone and the 87- metre-high campanile stands out as a beacon. The interior is 110 metres long and 36 metres to the top of the domes giving a feeling of massive magnificence. Eric Gill's relief of the Stations of the Cross is considered an outstanding modern work of art.

Mit dem Bau von **Westminster Cathedral** für die römisch-katholische Kirche wurde 1895 begonnen. Sie wurde von John Francis Bentley im byzantinischen Stil entworfen. Ihr auffallendes Äußeres aus roten Ziegelsteinen ist mit Streifen aus weißem Stein durchsetzt, und die 87 meter hohe Kampanile überragt ihre Umgebung wie ein Leuchtturm.

La cathédrale de Westminster pour les fidèles catholiques fut commencée en 1895 et dessinée par John Francis Bentley dans le style byzantin. L'alternance de la brique rouge et de la pierre blanche lui confère un aspect très distinctif, encore rehaussé par le campanile de 87 mètres de haut qui se détache comme un phare.

Buckingham Palace was built in 1703 and bought by King George III sixty years later. The sumptuous State Apartments are used for investitures and entertaining visiting heads of state.

Outside the Palace, at 11.30 on summer mornings and on alternate days in winter, the Changing of the Guard ceremony takes place accompanied by Guards' bands. The Royal Family occupies the north wing and the Royal Standard flies over the Palace when the Queen is in residence.

Buckingham Palace wurde 1703 erbaut und sechzig Jahre später von König Georg III. gekauft. Die Prunkzimmer werden für Auszeichnungszeremonien und den Empfang von Staatsoberhäuptern verwendet.

Im Sommer um 11.30 Uhr und im Winter an jedem zweiten Tag findet vor dem Palast die Wachablösung, das "Changing of the Guards", unter Begleitung der Gardekapellen statt. Die königliche Familie bewohnt den Nordflügel des Palastes. Wenn die Königin anwesend ist, fliegt die königliche Flagge auf dem Palast.

Le palais de Buckingham fut construit en 1703 et acquis soixante ans plus tard par le roi Georges III. Les somptueux salons d'apparat sont destinés aux cérémonies d'investiture et à recevoir les chefs d'Etat au cours de leur visite officielle.

Dans l'avant-cour du Palais, à 11h30 les matins d'été et tous les deux jours en hiver, se déroule la cérémonie de la relève de la garde au son de la fanfare des gardes. La famille royale occupe l'aile nord du palais et on hisse l'étendard royal quand la reine est en résidence.

The area of St James's is named after a 13th century hospital for lepers. King Henry VIII in the 16th century ordered the land to be cleared and a royal palace to be built on the site. The only Tudor remains today are the gate house and chapel.

It is to the Court of St James today that all foreign ambassadors still present their credentials. **St James's Palace** is now the office of the Lord Chamberlain's department.

Der Bezirk St James's ist nach einem Krankenhaus für Leprakranke benannt, das sich im 13. Jahrhundert hier befand. König Heinrich VIII befahl im 16. Jahrhundert die Räumung des Geländes und den Bau eines Königspalastes. Die einzigen Überreste aus der Tudorzeit sind heute das Pförtnerhaus und die Kapelle. Die Deckengemälde in der Kapelle sind wahrscheinlich von Holbein. Heute noch legen alle ausländischen Botschafter ihre Papiere dem Hof von St James vor.

Le quartier de St. James doit son nom à un hôpital du 13e siècle pour les lépreux. Au 16e siècle, le roi Henri VIII ordonna de défricher les terres et de construire un palais royal sur ce site. Les seuls vestiges de l'époque des Tudor qui restent encore aujourd'hui sont le corps-de-garde et la chapelle dont on pense qu'Holbein avait peint le plafond. C'est à la Cour St. James que tous les ambassadeurs étrangers viennent présenter leurs lettres de créance.

Named to commemorate Admiral Lord Nelson's great naval victory over the French in 1805, **Trafalgar Square** is a traditional rendezvous for pigeons and political rallies.

Four bronze lions, cast from cannon from a sunken ship, lie at the feet of the column from which Nelson gazes towards the Houses of Parliament in the distance.

Trafalgar Square wurde zum Andenken an den großen Marinesieg von Admiral Lord Nelson über Frankreich im Jahre 1805 benannt und ist ein für die Veranstaltung politischer Demonstrationen - und bei Tauben - beliebter Ort. Am Fuß der Säule, von der die Statue des Admirals zu den Houses of Parliament blickt, liegen vier Bronzelöwen, die aus eingeschmolzenen Kanonen von einem gesunkenen Schiff gegossen wurden.

Nommée pour commémorer la grande bataille navale de Lord Nelson en 1805 contre les Français, **Trafalgar Square** est le grand lieu de rendez-vous des pigeons et des manifestations politiques. Quatre lions en bronze, coulés dans le métal des canons d'un navire coulé, montent la garde au pied de la colonne d'où Nelson contemple au loin le Parlement.

Founded in 1735, the **British Museum** is a treasure house of the works of man from prehistoric times to the present day. There are important displays of antiquities from Egypt, Western Asia, Greece, Rome and the East. Notable exhibits include 13th century Magna Carta, William Shakespeare's first folio published in 1623; the Lindisfarne Gospels; the Parthenon sculptures; the Rosetta Stone; Egyptian mummies; the Lewis Chessmen and the Sutton Hoo treasure.

The building, begun in 1824, was designed by Robert Smirke and took 30 years to complete.

Das British Museum wurde 1735 gegründet. Es ist eine Schatzkammer menschlichen Schaffens von der prähistorischen Zeit bis in die Gegenwart. Hier findet man wichtige Altertümer aus Ägypten, Westasien, Griechenland, Rom und dem Osten. Zu den bemerkenswertesten Gegenständen gehört die Magna Carta aus dem 13. Jahrhundert, William Shakespeares erster Foliant, der 1623 veröffentlicht wurde, die Lindisfarne-Evangelien, die Parthenon-Skulpturen, der Rosetta-Stein, ägyptische Mumien, die "Lewis Chessmen" und der Sutton Hoo Schatz.

Fondé en 1735, le **British Museum** abrite une collection des oeuvres de l'homme depuis la préhistoire à nos jours. Il regroupe de remarquables objets venus d'Egypte, d'Asie mineure, de Grèce, de Rome et de l'Orient. Parmi ses trésors figurent Magna Carta du 13e siècle; le premier manuscrit de William Shakespeare en 1623; les évangiles de Lindisfarne; les sculptures du Parthénon; la pierre de Rosette; des momies égyptiennes; le trésor de Lewis Chessmen et de Sutton Hoo.

One man's energy and enterprise produced the cluster of ***museums*** in Kensington.

Prince Albert, consort to Queen Victoria, proposed that profits from a great exhibition of British work in 1851 be used to build them.

Die Ansammlung ***der Museen*** in Kensington entstand durch die Energie und die Initiative eines einzigen Mannes. Prinz Albert, Prinzgemahl Königin Victorias, schlug vor, daß die Gewinne von einer großen britischen Ausstellung im Jahr 1851 zum Bau dieser Museen verwendet werden sollten.

Le dynamisme et l'initiative d'un homme produisirent le groupe ***de musées*** de Kensington. Le Prince Albert, prince consort de la reine Victoria, proposa que les bénéfices de la Grande Exposition des exemples de l'artisanat britannique de 1851 soient versés pour les construire.

The Royal Albert Hall in Kensington is the home of good music, from classical to pop. Opened in 1871, this immense structure was modelled on Roman amphitheatres.

A terracotta frieze around the outside celebrates the triumph of arts and letters. Inside can be found one of the mightiest organs in the world with more than 9,000 pipes.

A series of promenade concerts is held each summer in the Hall.

Die Royal Albert Hall in Kensington ist Heimat guter Musik, von klassischen Stücken bis zu Pop. Dieses riesige ovale Bauwerk wurde römischen Amphitheatern nachgestaltet und 1871 fertiggestellt.

Ein Terrakotta-Fries an seiner Außenseite feiert den Triumpf von Kunst und Schrift.

Im Inneren der Royal Albert Hall befindet sich eine der gewaltigsten Orgeln der Welt mit über 9.000 Pfeifen.

Le Royal Albert Hall, à Kensington, est le sanctuaire de la bonne musique, de la musique classique à la musique "pop". Inaugurée en 1871, cette immense structure ovale fut inspirée des amphithéâtres romains.

Une frise en argile cuite encercle l'extérieur pour célébrer le triomphe des arts et des lettres.

A l'intérieur, se trouve l'une des plus puissantes orgues du monde avec plus de 9.000 tuyaux.

Kensington is one of London's royal boroughs. Many members of today's royal family continue the tradition by making it their London base.

The palace was built for a member of the British aristocracy and bought by King William III in 1689. He then employed Sir Christopher Wren to rebuild it and the south wing of the red brick palace is the notable surviving part of his work.

The State Apartments were restored and opened to the public in 1975.

Kensington ist einer der königlichen Bezirke von London. Viele Mitglieder der königlichen Familie setzen die Tradition, Kensington zu ihrer Londoner Heimat zu machen, auch heute noch fort.

Der Palast wurde für ein Mitglied des britischen Adels gebaut und 1689 von König Wilhelm III. gekauft. Er beauftragte Sir Christopher Wren mit seinem Umbau. Der Südflügel des Palastes aus roten Ziegelsteinen ist der wesentliche noch vorhandene Teil von Wrens Werk.

Kensington est l'un des "royal boroughs" (communes royales) de Londres. De nombreux membres de la famille royale continuent la tradition en en faisant leur lieu de résidence à Londres.

Le palais fut construit pour un membre de l'aristocratie britannique et acquis par le roi Guillaume III en 1689. Il fit alors appel à Sir Christopher Wren pour le reconstruire et l'aile sud de ce palais en briques rouges est le vestige le plus évocateur de son oeuvre.

On the north bank of the Thames at Millbank is **Tate Britain**. Opened in 1897, the classical fronted building was commissioned by the sugar tycoon Sir Henry Tate. Today the gallery houses a comprehensive display of British art from the 16th century to the present day, including masterpieces by Reynolds, Gainsborough, Constable and the Pre-Raphaelites. The Clore Gallery is a separate wing dedicated to the works of Turner.

The original collection included modern art, which is now displayed in Tate Modern on Bankside.

Am Millbank am Nordufer der Themse befindet sich **Tate Britain**. Dieses 1897 eröffnete Geböude mit seiner klassizistischen Fassade wurde vom Zuckermagnaten Sir Henry Tate in Auftrag gegeben. Heute beherbergt die Galerie eine eindrucksvolle Ausstellung britischer Kunst vom 16. Jahrhundert bis zur Gegenwart, die Meisterwerke von Reynolds, Gainsborough, Constable und Werke der Präraffaeliten umfasst. Die Clore Gallery ist ein separater, den Werken Turners gewidmeter Flügel.

Die Originalsammlung schloss moderne Kunst ein. Diese wird jetzt in der Tate Modern am Bankside ausgestellt.

Sur la rive nord de la Tamise, à Millbank, se trouve la **Tate Britain**. Inauguré en 1897, ce bâtiment à façade classique fut commandé par le magnat du sucre, Sir Henry Tate. De nos jours, ce musée abrite une collection étendue d'art britannique, due XVIe siècle à nos jours, avec des œuvres de Reynolds, Gainsborough, Constable et des préraphaélites. La galerie Clore est une aile séparée, consacrée aux úuvres de Turner.

La collection d'origine comprenait des œuvres d'art moderne, aujourd'hui exposées à la Tate Modern, sur Bankside.

Housed in the former Bedlam asylum building for the insane, the ***Imperial War Museum*** is a collection covering 20th century warfare. As well as planes, tanks, weaponry - even a submarine - it contains the personal mementoes of those affected by war. Striking paintings and posters vividly depict battle scenes.

The museum now features reconstructions of the London blitz and World War I trenches, where visitors can experience for themselves the sights, sounds and circumstances of wartime.

Das ***Imperial War Museum*** befindet sich in einer ehemaligen Bedlam-Anstalt für Geisteskranke. Seine Sammlung umfaßt die Kriegskunst des 20. Jahrhunderts. Neben Flugzeugen, Panzern, Waffen - sogar einem U-Boot - enthält es die persönlichen Andenken der vom Krieg Betroffenen. Beeindruckende Gemälde und Poster lassen Kampfszenen lebendig werden.

Das Museum enthält jetzt auch Rekonstruktionen der Bombenangriffe auf London und der Schützengräben des ersten Weltkriegs. Hier können Besucher die Umstände und Bedingungen von Kriegssituationen optisch und akustisch selbst erfahren.

Logé dans l'ancien asyle Bedlam pour les fous, ***l'Imperial War Museum*** abrite une collection couvrant les guerres du 20e siècle. En plus d'avions, de tanks, d'armes, et même un sous-marin, il contient les souvenirs personnels de ceux affectés par la guerre. Des tableaux et des affiches remarquables dépeignent avec force les scènes des batailles.

Ce musée présente aussi des reconstructions du Blitz de Londres et des tranchées de la Première Guerre Mondiale, où les visiteurs peuvent ressentir pour eux-mêmes les scènes, les sons et les circonstances de la guerre.

The mention of the name **Wimbledon** anywhere will immediately result in it being recognised as the home of lawn tennis, the site of the most prestigious tournament in the world.

The first Lawn Tennis championship was staged in 1877.

In 1997 the new No 1 Court was used for the first time, replacing the old No 1 Court which was opened in 1924.

One interesting statistic from Wimbledon is that an average of 32,000 tennis balls are used during the course of the Championships each year.

Wimbledon ist überall als die Heimat des Rasentennis bekannt - als Veranstaltungsort des renommiertesten Turniers der Welt.

Die ersten Rasentennis-Meisterschaften fanden 1877 statt.

Der alte Platz 1, der 1924 eröffnet wurde, wird 1997 durch den neuen Platz 1 ersetzt.

Dès que le nom de **Wimbledon** est mentionné quelque part, il évoque immédiatement le foyer du tennis sur gazon, le terrain où se déroulent les tournois les plus prestigieux du monde.

Le premier championnat de tennis sur gazon fut organisé en 1877.

En 1997, le Court N 1 qui remplace l'ancien Court N 1 ouvert en 1924, sera mis à l'épreuve pour la première fois.

What was started as a modest gardening hobby by a Princess in 1759 has grown into the world's most famous and extensive collection of plants and flowers. Known formally as the **Royal Botanical Gardens** at Kew, the natural greenery and scenery is enhanced by temples, follies and the ten storey pagoda.

Kew's architecural glories are the 19th century greenhouses designed by Decimus Burton. The latest and largest plant house is the Princess of Wales Conservatory opened in 1987. It features 10 computer controlled world "climates" and their associated vegetation. Kew's most important function today is as a scientific institution.

Was 1759 als ein bescheidenes Gärtnerhobby einer Prinzessin begann, ist zu einer der berühmtesten und umfassendsten Sammlung von Pflanzen und Blumen der Welt herangewachsen. Die natürlichen Grünanlågen und Formen des Parks, der offiziell als **"Royal Botanical Gardens** at Kew" bekannt ist, werden durch Tempel, Pavillons und eine zehnstöckige Pagode verziert.

Die architektonische Pracht von Kew sind die von Decimus Burton entworfenen Gewächshäuser aus dem 19. Jahrhundert. Das neueste und größte Pflanzenhaus ist das Princess of Wales Conservatory, das 1987 eröffnet wurde.

Ce qui, à l'origine n'était qu'un modeste passe-temps de jardinage d'une princesse en 1759, est devenu l'une des collections les plus célèbres et les plus complètes de plantes et de fleurs du monde. Connu officiellement sous le nom de **Royal Botanical Gardens** à Kew, la verdure et les paysages naturels sont égayés par des temples, des gloriettes et une pagode de dix étages.

Les splendeurs architecturales de Kew sont les serres du 19e siècle dessinées par Decimus Burton. La dernière serre qui est la plus grande est le conservatoire de la Princesse de Galles inauguré en 1987.

Hampton Court by the River Thames was the grandest of all houses built in Britain in the 16th century. It was seized from Cardinal Wolsey by King Henry VIII who moved into it with his new mistress, Anne Boleyn. The King then spent large amounts of money on improvements, including a closed tennis court, bowling alleys and a tiltyard for jousting tournaments. King Henry also ordered the Great Hall to be rebuilt, the chapel completed and new royal lodgings to be constructed. The palace was much loved by subsequent monarchs, though William and Mary, proclaimed king and queen in 1689, felt extensive modernisation was needed. Architect Sir Christopher Wren was brought in to remodel Hampton Court for them into a palace as lavish and stylish as Versailles.

The palace has 1,000 rooms and its treasures include paintings, furniture and tapestries.

Hampton Court an der Themse war das prächtigste aller im 16. Jahrhundert in Großbritannien erbauten Häuser. König Heinrich VIII beschlagnahmte es von Kardinal Wolsey und zog mit seiner neuen Geliebten, Anne Boleyn, ein. Der König gab dann riesige Summen für Verbesserungen aus. Der Palast war bei nachfolgenden Monarchen ebenfalls sehr beliebt. Wilhelm und Maria, die 1689 zum König und zur Königin gekrönt wurden, waren jedoch der Meinung, daß Hampton Court umfassend modernisiert werden müßte. Der Architekt Sir Christopher Wren wurde von ihnen mit der Umgestaltung von Hampton Court zu einem in Prunk und Eleganz dem Schloß in Versailles gleichenden Palast beauftragt.

Hampton Court, sur les bords de la Tamise, fut la plus magnifique de toutes les demeures construites en Grande-Bretagne au 16e siècle. Le roi Henri VIII la reprit au cardinal Wolsey. Il y emménagea avec sa nouvelle maîtresse, Anne Boleyn. Le roi engloutit d'énormes sommes d'argent pour l'améliorer. Le palais devint le palais royal préféré des monarques successifs, bien que Guillaume et Mary, proclamés roi et reine en 1689, trouvèrent le besoin de le faire complètement moderniser. Ils firent appel à l'architecte Sir Christopher Wren pour le transformer à leur goût, en un palais aussi somptueux et élégant que Versailles.

Windsor, the largest inhabited castle in the world, has been a royal home for 900 years. It was one of the first sites chosen by William the Conqueror as a massive link in a chain of fortresses he wanted to build around London to secure his newly acquired kingdom. Building started in 1070 on a high chalk cliff above the river Thames. In size and plan, the original castle is identical to the present structure.

Windsor has become a centre for the best of British craftmanship, from 17th century carving by Grinling Gibbons, to the exclusive Queen Mary's dolls' house and contents - strictly made to a scale of one twelfth life size. St George's Chapel, dedicated to the patron saint of England, is the chapel of the Knights of the Garter. It is a masterpiece of Perpendicular Gothic architecture with elaborately carved stone vaulting.

Visitors to the castle can view once again the magnificent State Apartments, painstakingly restored following fire damage in 1992.

Windsor ist die größte bewohnte Burg der Welt und schon seit 900 Jahren eine königliche Wohnung. Windsor war einer der ersten Orte, die von Wilhelm dem Eroberer als ein massives Glied in einer Kette von Festungen gewählt wurde, die er zur Sicherung seines neuerworbenen Königreiches um London herum bauen wollte. Mit dem Bau wurde 1070 auf einer hohen Kreideklippe über der Themse begonnen. In Größe und Grundriß ist die heutige Burg noch mit der ursprünglichen identisch.

Die Besucher des Schlosses können nun wieder die wunderschönen Staatsgemächer bewundern, die nach dem Brand 1992 sorgfältig wieder hergerichtet wurden.

Windsor, le plus vaste château habité du monde, est une résidence royale depuis 900 ans. C'était l'un des premiers sites choisi par Guillaume le Conquérant comme énorme maillon d'une chaîne de forteresses qu'il voulait construire pour encercler Londres afin de consolider son royaume nouvellement acquis. Sa construction commença en 1070 sur une haute falaise de craie dominant la Tamise. Du point de vue de sa taille et de son plan, le château original était identique à la structure actuelle.

Les magnifiques appartements officiels, minutieusement restaurés après qu'un incendie les eut détruits en 1992, sont à nouveau ouverts au public.

Eton College, the most famous school in the world, was founded in 1440 by King Henry VI to provide free education to 70 scholars.

Eton, just across the river from Windsor, still offers 70 scholarships but the ancient buildings of the College now house nearly 1300 boys. Tradition and custom play a huge part in life at the public school that has educated so many distinguished and eminent men.

Visitors can take guided tours of the College where a museum gives an insight into life at Eton over the centuries.

Eton College, die berühmteste Schule der Welt, wurde 1440 von Heinrich VI. gegründet, um 70 Stipendiaten kostenlose Schulbildung zu gewähren.

Das direkt gegenüber von Windsor am Themseufer befindliche Eton vergibt noch immer 70 Stipendien, jedoch berherbergen die uralten College-Gebäude jetzt fast 1300 Knaben. Tradition und Brauchtum spielen noch immer eine gewaltige Rolle im Leben der Privatschule, die so viele namhafte Männer ausbildete.

Besucher können geführte Rundgänge durch das College unternehmen, und ein Museum verschafft ihnen Einblick in das Leben in Eton im Lauf der Jahrhunderte.

Eton, le collège le plus renommé dans le monde, fut fondé en 1440 par le roi Henri VI, pour donner une éducation gratuite à 70 étudiants.

Situé face à Windsor, de l'autre côté de la Tamise, le collège d'Eton propose toujours 70 bourses d'étude, mais les bâtiments anciens du collège accueillent aujourd'hui près de 1 300 garçons. La tradition et les coutumes jouent un grand rôle dans la vie de cet établissement privé, où tant d'hommes distingués ont fait leurs études.

Les visiteurs peuvent faire une visite guidée du collège, qui contient un musée donnant un aperçu de la vie à Eton au cours des siècles.